1. H1417 served as a prototype for the Bristol Fighter Mk. IV conversions of Mk. IIIs made in 1928. A further increase in loaded weight necessitated additional strengthening of the structure and a sturdier undercarriage, while to improve handling a revised fin and horn-balanced rudder were fitted, together with Handley Page slots on the upper wing. On H1417 alone these were linked to the ailerons, and the upper wings had square tips. (Bristol Aeroplane Co.)

VINTAGE WARBIRDS No 4

The Bristol Fighter

J. M. BRUCE

ARMS AND ARMOUR PRESS

Introduction

Published in 1985 by Arms and Armour Press
2-6 Hampstead High Street, London NW3 1QQ.

Distributed in the United States by
Sterling Publishing Co. Inc., 2 Park Avenue,
New York, N.Y. 10016.

British Library Cataloguing in Publication Data:
Bruce, Jack
The Bristol fighter. – (Vintage warbirds; no. 4)
1. Bristol F-2B (Fighter plane) – History
1. Title   II. Series
623.74′64   UG1242.F5
ISBN 0-85368-704-8

Editing, design and artwork by Roger Chesneau.
Typesetting by Typesetters (Birmingham) Ltd.
Printed and bound in Italy.

The Bristol Fighter had its origins in a Royal Flying Corps request, made in the autumn of 1915, for a two-seat corps-reconnaissance and artillery-spotting aircraft capable of defending itself. To meet this requirement, Frank S. Barnwell, chief designer of the British & Colonial Aeroplane Company, drew up the Bristol R2A, an equal-span two-seat tractor biplane with a 120hp Beardmore engine. He revised it, as the R2B, to accept the new 150hp Hispano-Suiza, changing to an unequal-span configuration but retaining the mid-gap fuselage position, close back-to-back crew positions and the characteristic tail unit. A further redesign for the bigger and more powerful 190hp Rolls-Royce Mk. I, later named Falcon I, produced the two-bay, equal-span Bristol F2A, and it was in this form that the design was built, and first flown, in 1916.

The F2A's operational début was disastrous – many were lost in early combats because at first no one knew how to exploit the Bristol's still unrecognized potential – but once pilots learned to fly the aircraft as a fighter, with primary offensive employment of the front gun, its success was assured. This success was consolidated in the improved F2B, which saw extensive and outstandingly effective employment in France, Palestine and Italy.

After the entry of the United States into the war in April 1917, the Bristol Fighter was one of the British aircraft types chosen for production in America. The extensive American redesign of the F2B to take the Liberty 12 engine created a new, much heavier, and substantially different aircraft, the USA O-1, and it – not the Bristol Fighter proper – proved to be a failure. A belated American decision to revert to the basic design with the 300hp Hispano-Suiza, which could and should have been taken earlier, came too late for production to get under way before the war ended. After the war, the air services of Belgium, Canada, the Irish Free State, Mexico, New Zealand, Norway, Peru, Poland and Spain all acquired Bristols, and variants and derivatives gave versatile service in many parts of the world.

With the postwar Royal Air Force, in squadrons all but crippled by Treasury parsimony, the Bristol remained in service until 1931, much modified, cruelly overloaded (for it was never to have any engine other than the Falcon III in RAF service), but gallantly willing – a fighter to the end. Its employment, on so-called army co-operation duties, was far removed in place and nature from its combat triumphs so valiantly won in the war-sundered skies of France, Italy and Palestine. Its ground-attack work against hapless tribesmen still demanded great skill and courage of its crews but made a crude bludgeon of a weapon that, in its time and in the right hands, had the precision and deadliness of a rapier.

The author gratefully acknowledges his indebtedness to several organizations and many individuals for photographs reproduced in this book. First among these is Stuart Leslie, whose help, as always, goes far beyond mere numbers of invaluable illustrations. Others to whom thanks are extended are Sqn. Ldr. R. C. B. Ashworth RAF (ret), Chaz Bowyer, A. E. Ferko, R. Gerrard, P. H. T. Green, E. Harlin, Sqn. Ldr. C. G. Jefford, Egon Krueger, K. M. Molson, D. R. Neate, Flt. Lt. A. S. Thomas and D. P. Woodhall. Major contributions have also come from Peter Liddle's 1914–18 Personal Experience Archives in Sunderland Polytechnic, the photographic archives of the former Bristol Aeroplane Company, the Royal Aircraft Establishment at Farnborough, the Royal Air Force Museum, Hendon, and the National Air & Space Museum, Washington, DC. Advice and information given by L. A. Rogers and Bruce Robertson have also been of great value in the compilation of the captions.

J. M. Bruce

◀2
2. In June 1924, Bristol Fighter C4654 was fitted at the RAE with this so-called tropical radiator, a designation that cannot readily be reconciled with the blanking-off of parts of the visible radiator. Nevertheless, the radiator cowl appears to have been dispensed with, and the external plumbing on the starboard side might have led to a retractable supplementary radiator. (RAE)

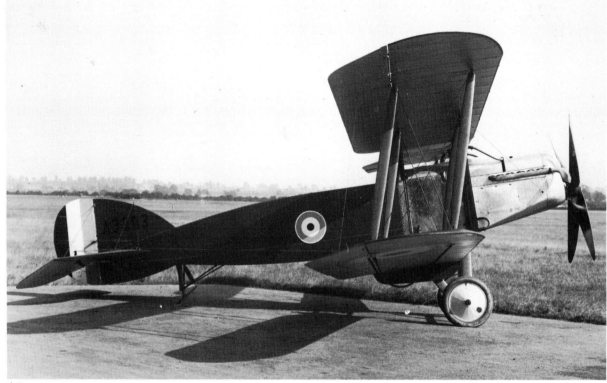

▲3

3. Two prototype Bristol F2As (A3303–3304) and fifty production aircraft (A3305–3354) were ordered. A3303, which first flew on 9 September 1916, had the 190hp Rolls-Royce Mk. I engine in a bulky and unprepossessing cowling, flanked by two tall radiator blocks. Both prototypes had modified BE2d main-planes, and the lower centre-section was an open, cross-braced frame, with endplates at the roots of the lower wings. (Bristol Aeroplane Co.)

4. Essentially as originally completed, A3303 first went to the Central Flying School (CFS) at Upavon for official performance and handling trials in September 1916. It still lacked a proper ring mounting for the observer's Lewis gun, and this photograph illustrates how high and relatively exposed the pilot's position was.

5, 6. The extent to which the tall radiators obstructed the pilot's view in vital directions was unaccept-able in a military aeroplane that had fighting and reconnaissance as its functions. An entirely new cooling system was fitted to A3303, the essence of which was a roughly circular frontal radiator mounted immediately behind the airscrew. With the redesigned cowling and improved top decking, the pilot's forward view was enhanced. (Bristol Aeroplane Co.)

▼4

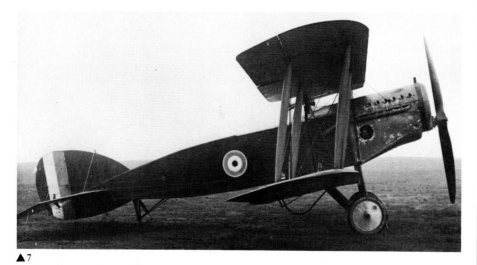

▲7

▲8

7. When A3303 returned to the CFS for further trials in October 1916, the end-plates had been removed from the lower wing roots. Its full official assessment was recorded in Report M.69; when tested it had engine No. 1/190/16 and its propeller on the tests was a four-blader, No. 3717. The aircraft subsequently went to the Armament Experimental Station at Orfordness for armament trials.

8, 9. At Orfordness, A3303 was fitted with the Constantinesco synchronizing system and an Aldis optical sight for the Vickers gun, and a Scarff ring mounting for the Lewis. Orfordness used it as a test vehicle, but on 7 July 1917 it pursued the 18 Gothas that had bombed London. Its pilot was Lt. F. D. Holder and the observer Lt. F. W. Musson, but they were unable to get within range of the German formation.

10. From the outset the 150hp Hispano-Suiza was regarded as an alternative power unit for the Bristol F2A. The second prototype, A3304, was completed by 25 October 1916, and it emerged with the Hispano-Suiza engine cleanly cowled behind a circular frontal radiator. This second F2A differed from A3303 in having a close coaming about the pilot's cockpit and its tailskid built into the base of the rudder. (Bristol Aeroplane Co.)

11. The Bristol F2A's upper longerons ran horizontally from the cockpits to the engine firewall, producing a form that cut off an important area of the pilot's forward view. To improve this, the longerons were angled downwards from the rear of the pilot's cockpit to the engine bearers, and the top decking tapered upwards. This modification was made on A3304 and tested at the CFS on 4 and 6 December 1916. (Bristol Aeroplane Co.)

▼9

▲12　▼13

14▲

◀15

12. All production F2As had the 190hp Rolls-Royce Mk. I (Falcon I) engine, fitted with a larger radiator than that of A3303, together with redesigned engine cowling panels. New wings with blunt tips replaced the BE2d wings of the prototypes, and a fully built-out lower centre-section, as on the modified A3304, was fitted. The radiator originally had a cambered cowling ring of appreciable chord, as seen here on A3312.

13. The first Bristol Fighter squadron was No. 48, which went to France on 8 March 1917, and its early operational experience with the F2A was unhappy. The Bristol's crews did not at first handle it as a true fighter, and combat losses were consequently heavy. A3322 (2nd Lt. H. D. Davies, 2nd Lt. R. S. Worsley) was brought down intact on 13 April 1917 either by *Leutnant* Simon or *Leutnant* Lothar von Richthofen, of *Jasta 11*. (A. E. Ferko)

14. At an early stage the radiator cowling was cut back, presumably to improve cooling. A3345 was officially allocated to the Royal Flying Corps (RFC) with the Expeditionary Force on 5 March 1917, and in this photograph, dated 23 March, is seen at No. 2 Aircraft Depot, Candas, with its radiator cowling cropped. This F2A was flown back to England on 12 June 1917.

15. This close-up of the nose of A3329 shows how the elimination of the cambered portion of the radiator cowling reduced its chord. Also visible are the drive to the generator of the Constantinesco gun-synchronizing system and the circular aperture in the radiator through which the Vickers gun fired. (Chaz Bowyer)

11

▲16

▲17 ▼18

16. The pilot of the Bristol F2A was not distracted by a multiplicity of instruments, for they were so few that there was not even an instrument panel. In this photograph the central and most prominent feature is the Vickers gun, its Type A trigger motor lethally placed to ensure facial injury to the pilot in the event of a crash. On later aircraft special padding was fitted over the trigger motor. (RAF Museum)

17. This photograph of the F2A forward fuselage clearly shows the wide and angular cross-section of the upper decking ahead of the pilot. To left of centre is the Aldis optical sight, to starboard the ring and bead sights, between which lay an access panel to the belt-feed and ammunition box for the Vickers gun. (RAF Museum)

18. One or two F2As, including the first prototype A3303, served as experimental hacks at the Armament Experimental Station, Orfordness. This photograph illustrates an experimental mechanism devised at Orfordness as a wind-balancing attachment to the observer's Scarff ring. It was tested with both a single Lewis gun and the double-yoked pair seen here.

19. All Bristol Fighters from A7101 onwards were designated F2B, having the modified fuselage tested on A3304 and the full-aerofoil lower centre-section. The inclined upper longerons permitted the introduction of a larger upper fuel tank and ammunition box for the Vickers gun. The earliest production F2Bs retained the 190hp Rolls-Royce Mk. I, the form of the engine cowling being such that the water pipes to the cylinder blocks protruded through cut-outs. A7107 exhibits these features in this photograph, taken when it was aircraft '6' of the Wireless Experimental Establishment at Biggin Hill and had a wind-driven generator fitted under the lower centre-section. It had earlier seen operational service with No. 48 Squadron.

20, 21. At a relatively early stage in F2B production the small apertures on the upper engine cowling above the exhaust manifold were replaced by an elongated air intake, seen here in these fine studies of A7135. The apparent reversal of the colours in the roundels and rudder stripes is intriguing. This aircraft was at one time with No. 35 Training Squadron at Northolt and took part in at least three Home Defence actions. (RAF Museum)

BRISTOL FIGHTER

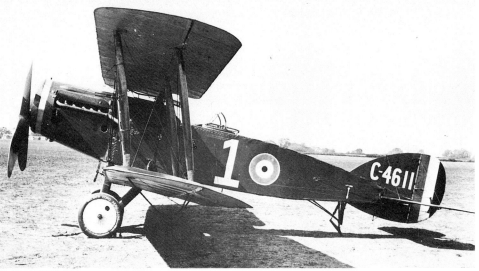

22. As the Rolls-Royce Falcon was developed through the 220hp Mk. II to the 275hp Mk. III, these engines were fitted to later Bristol Fighters, somewhat haphazardly according to availability. The subject aircraft for performance tests with the Falcon II was A7183, which went to Martlesham Heath on 25 July 1917 and subsequently to Orfordness on 10 August. This photograph shows the aircraft fitted with navigation lights. (P. Liddle)

23. The Falcon III's carburettors were placed ahead of the cylinder banks instead of between them as on the Falcon Is and IIs, and consequently the radiator had to be mounted slightly further forward and the cowling elongated. Later F2Bs that had to make do with Falcon I or II engines usually had the Falcon III cowling and radiator position and were externally indistinguishable unless one of the relatively few left-hand Falcon Is or IIs was fitted (there were no left-hand Falcon IIIs). C4611 (Falcon III) of the Wireless Experimental Establishment, Biggin Hill, had a four-bladed propeller of Type A.M.2451, diameter 2,670mm.

24. C4814, although an operational aircraft of No. 11 Squadron, was reported as having a Falcon I. It was at Bristol Aircraft Acceptance Park, allocated to the RFC in France, on 31 October 1917, and was flown back to England on 12 December 1917. (Chaz Bowyer)

25. B1125 (Falcon II) was reported to be at Bristol AAP when it was allocated to the RFC in France on 20 September 1917. It went to No. 20 Squadron but fell into enemy hands seemingly intact, as this post-capture photograph shows. Its pilot and observer were Lt. W. D. Chambers and 2nd Lt. F. H. Berry, reported missing on 8 October 1917 on a special reconnaissance of the Roulers-Menin area. See also photograph 43. (A. E. Ferko)

26. One of the most successful Bristol Fighter squadrons was No. 22, which re-equipped from FE2bs in July 1917. One of its early Bristols was A7163, which had been completed and allocated to the RFC in France by 16 June 1917. It survived its operational career and was flown back to England on 17 March 1918. This photograph is believed to have been taken, possibly at Dover, by Capt. J. T. B. McCudden MC MM.

27. B1134 had the Falcon II and was one of the very few Falcon-powered Bristol F2Bs that went to corps squadrons. It had first been assigned to the RFC in France on 24 September 1917 and was issued to No. 48 Squadron. It was attached to No. 35 Squadron, an Armstrong Whitworth FK8 unit, on 4 February 1918, and is here seen in No. 35's markings.

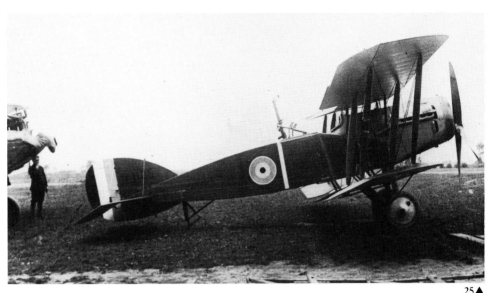

25▲

26▲   27▼

▲28

28. In December 1917 lengthened exhaust pipes were introduced, and in January 1918 official instructions required these to be fitted as a Class II modification. The first form is seen here on an aircraft of No. 11 Squadron that bears the intriguing name 'Rickadamdoo'. The pilot is Lt. A. P. Maclean and his observer Lt. F. H. Cantlon – both Canadians. (K. M. Molson)

29. The instrument panel of the F2B was somewhat better furnished than that of the F2A, and the trigger motor of the Vickers gun was clad in a neat if somewhat ungenerously padded sleeve to reassure pilots. The tapered form of the top decking can be seen.

▼29

30, 31. These two photos give some impression of the view from the pilot's cockpit and, more importantly, the remarkable contours of the top decking, shaped to minimize restriction of the pilot's forward view. The Aldis optical sight was underslung below the upper centre-section on a special mounting. Forward vision was always critical, and the introduction of an enlarged radiator for the Falcon III in May 1918 led to protests from the squadrons, for it was 3in higher and obscured part of the object field of the Aldis sight. The aircraft in the second photograph has a Thornton Pickard camera gun for training purposes. (RAF Museum)

▲32

▲33　▼34

32. C4619 (Falcon III) went to France with No. 62 Squadron on 29 January 1918, flown by Captain W. E. Staton MC DFC★ and Lt. J. R. Gordon (here standing by the aircraft), who shot down several enemy aircraft. Staton's victory score eventually totalled 25½ and Gordon's 4, all won on Bristols. C4619, its duty gallantly done, was flown back to England on 28 July 1918. (D. R. Neate)
33. Various individual attempts were made by pilots to augment the Bristol's forward-firing armament. One installation made on more than one F2B was an elevated adaptation of a Foster mounting fitted above the centre-section and offset to starboard of centre. E2586 was a late-production, Bristol-built F2B of No. 11 Squadron that retained its overwing Lewis gun after the Armistice, and is here seen at Nivelles in 1919. (K. M. Molson)
34. In Palestine the Bristol F2B flew and fought with No. 67 Squadron (No. 1 Squadron, Australian Flying Corps) and No. 111,

which shared Ramleh airfield. A7194 (Falcon I) has been reported as having seen service with both squadrons, and is known to have been with No. 111 in October 1917. (Chaz Bowyer)
35. One of the great fighting teams of No. 67 Squadron (No. 1 Sqn AFC): Captain Ross ('Hadji') Smith, Lt. E. A. ('Pard') Mustard (later Mustar) and their Bristol, possibly B1229, a presentation aircraft ('Australia No. 12, New South Wales No. 11, the Macintyre Kayuga Estate'). Ross Smith was later knighted for his great flight from England to Australia in a Vimy, 12 November–10 December 1919.
36. Two F2Bs in Palestine. The nearer has a two-bladed type P.3033 propeller, the other (probably C4626, much used by No. 67 Squadron) a four-bladed type P.3045. The RFC in France found that the F2B's performance was better, but that the engine had a greater tendency to overheat, with the two-blader. (RAF Museum)

36▼

19

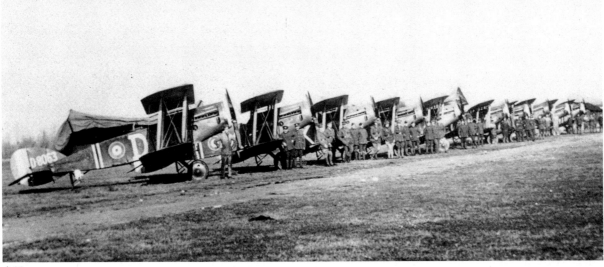

▲37

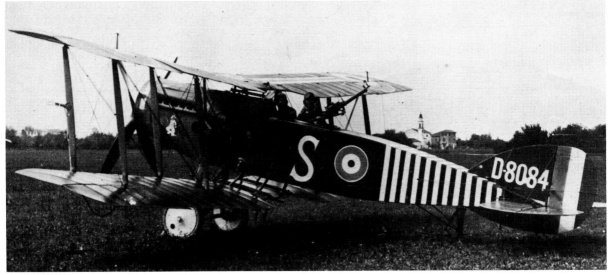

▲38   ▼39

37. No. 139 Squadron flew the Bristol Fighter in Italy. The F2Bs seen here are wearing the squadron's original markings of two white bands round the fuselage behind the roundel. (E. Harlin)

38. After Maj. W. G. Barker DSO★ MC★ assumed command of No. 139 Squadron on 14 July 1918, the fuselage markings of the unit's Bristols were elaborated to consist of an array of black and white bands. D8084, here seen at Villaverla, also bore spanwise white stripes on the upper wings and a cartoon of Charlie Chaplin on the engine cowling.

39. Just as B1134 had been attached to No. 35 Squadron RFC, so were two Bristol Fighters attached to No. 3 Squadron AFC late in September 1918. E2529 was one of these; its pilot was Capt. Lawrence J. Wackett, whose name became widely known in the Australian aircraft industry in later years.

40. The last of the Bristol Fighter squadrons to reach France before the Armistice was No. 88, which left Britain on 20 April 1918. It remained on the continent after the Armistice, disbanding at Nivelles on 10 August 1919. E2220 was, with seeming numerical inevitability, '22' of No. 88 Squadron. By September 1919 it was with No. 12 Squadron RAF, and it was crashed by Capt. P. F. Fullard DSO MC AFC on 23 December 1919.

41. No. 138 Squadron was mobilizing at Chingford as a Bristol Fighter squadron as the war ended. As at 31 October 1918, twenty F2Bs at Bristol Aircraft Acceptance Park had been allocated to No. 138 Squadron, among them F4580. (E. Harlin)

42. Although it was intended that the Long Range Artillery Spotting Flights should be equipped with Arab-powered Bristol Fighters, deliveries of these were belated and few, and some Falcon-powered F2Bs were issued to these flights. One such was F4306, here seen at Aulnoy; the aircraft was used by L Flight in France and later by No. 141 Squadron, presumably in Ireland.

40▲

41▲ **42▼**

▲43 ▼44

43. Inevitably a few Bristol Fighters fell into German hands intact or repairable. This one, possibly B1125 of No. 20 Squadron RFC (see photograph 25) was used as a communications aircraft by *Jasta* 5. (Egon Krueger)
44. A7231 was the F2B of No. 11 Squadron that was flown by Lts. E. Scholtz and H. C. Wookey, who were shot down by *Feldwebel* Karl Bey of *Jasta* 5 on 17 October 1917. Because their aircraft contained propaganda leaflets, Scholtz and Wookey were subjected to trial by a German court martial and sentenced to ten years hard labour. The supplication on the conspicuously repainted aircraft reads 'Don't shoot! Good people'. (Egon Krueger)
45. Wookey and Scholtz photographed with their captor, Karl Bey, in front of an Albatros DV, presumably of *Jasta* 5. (Egon Krueger)
46. The Bristol Fighter was introduced to the night-fighting role in September 1917 when No. 39 (Home Defence) Squadron began to re-equip with the type. This F2B of the squadron, C4636, flown by Lt. A. J. Arkell with Air Mechanic A. T. C. Stagg as his observer, shot down a Gotha on the night of 19/20 May 1918.

46▼

▲47

▲48 ▼49

47. C4636 was not painted in the normal PC10 finish, and various experiments in special night coloration were conducted at Orfordness and in the Home Defence squadrons. Here the Bristols of No. 141 (HD) Squadron display a variety of finishes. The cockerel marking on the fuselages symbolizes the squadron's gaining of the 'Cock Squadron' title in the VI Brigade's Squadron-at-Arms competition of 22 September 1918. (Chaz Bowyer)
48. Maj. (later Air Vice-Marshal Sir) Brian Baker DSO MC, Officer Commanding No. 141 Squadron, with E2604, which had a non-standard (perhaps NIVO) finish and its cockerel marking painted on the fin. (Sqn. Ldr. C. G. Jefford)
49. This, or a similarly clad, F2B was with No. 141 (HD) Squadron in 1918. Its finish appears to have been a multi-coloured pattern that closely resembled the German printed-pattern fabric. (A. J. Jackson)

50. Three Bristols of No. 39 (HD) Squadron, seemingly in PC10 finish but with the white elements of the national markings removed; the nearest aircraft is B1330 and the second C4650. All three have the special 45° installation of the Neame illuminated sight on the centre-section trailing edge, to which angle the observer aligned his Lewis guns for accurate upward firing at 100mph.

51. The Home Defence squadrons were less likely to be involved in frenetic dog-fighting and were therefore better able to augment their aircraft's armament with less regard to its effect on agility and perform-ance. This five-gun Bristol F2B, apparently of No. 39 (HD) Squadron and despite its possible indebtedness to Mr. Heath Robinson, speaks for itself. (RAF Museum)

52. The exposed interior of this Bristol of No. 48 Squadron reveals the installation of an air-driven camera, the stow-age of spare Lewis-gun magazines and signal cartridges, a small demolition charge, and the observer's confined accommodation. The aircraft has its extended exhaust pipes modified, perhaps to accord with the decision of 21 September 1918 that 'the outlet should be raised to a point midway between the top and bottom longerons'.

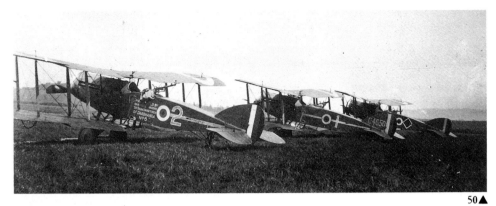

50▲

51▲   52▼

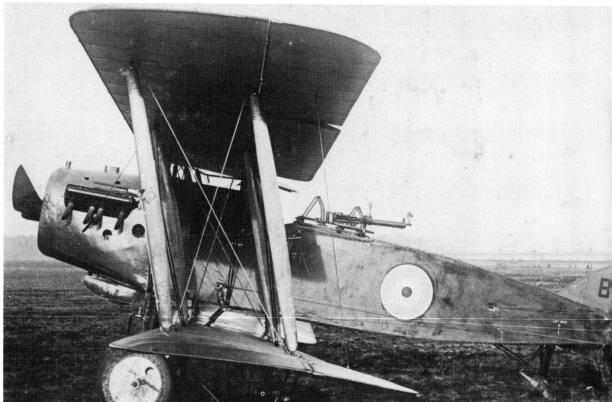

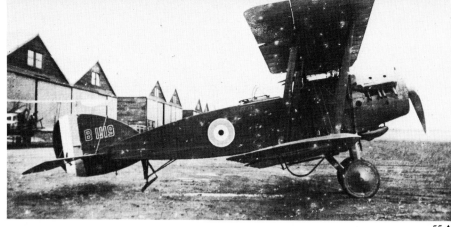

53. B1124 (Falcon II) was luckier than her captured contemporaries. This F2B was allocated to the RFC in France on 19 September 1917, went to No. 48 Squadron, and came down in Holland with engine failure on 29 September. Second Lts. F. L. Smith and J. Frost were interned and their aircraft taken over by the *Luchtvaart Afdeling* as BR401. It remained in Dutch service until 1924. (Bristol Aeroplane Co.)

54. When the F2B was chosen as a replacement for the RE8 and Armstrong Whitworth FK8, an alternative to the Falcon had to be found. The first choice was the 200hp Hispano-Suiza, and, thus powered, B1201 went to Martlesham Heath for trials on 31 December 1917. By 9 February 1918 its engine was in Sopwith Dolphin C3778 but presumably was replaced for B1201's transfer to Farnborough on 28 February. (RAF Museum)

55. Another of the early installations of the Hispano-Suiza was made in B1119, which went to France and was tested at No. 1 Aeroplane Supply Depot, St.-Omer, on 2 January 1918. It returned to Lympne on 24 January and was flown to the Southern Aircraft Repair Depot at Farnborough on 4 February. (P. H. T. Green)

56. Contemporary with the early Hispano-Suiza installations were one of a 230hp Beardmore-Halford-Pullinger in B7781, and another of a Siddeley Puma (seen here in a poor-quality but exceedingly rare photograph) in B1206; B7781 was tested at No. 1 Aeroplane Supply Depot on 10 and 13 January 1918, B1206 at Martlesham later that month. This F2B variant was intended to be an escort fighter but its performance was so poor that the idea was abandoned on 26 February. The Falcon radiator was retained. (RAF Museum)

▲ 57

57. Scarcity of Hispano-Suizas compelled the use of the 200hp Sunbeam Arab in the corps-reconnaissance version of the Bristol. The earliest installations were made by the Western Aircraft Repair Depot in reconstructed F2Bs B8914 and B8915, in a Falcon-type housing. B8915 arrived at Martlesham for testing on 8 February 1918. Six further Bristols were converted by the WARD, and several went to France in February 1918. (RAF Museum)

58. Twelve contracts for F2Bs, mostly with Arab engines, were given to eight additional contractors, but engine development troubles seriously delayed deliveries and the hoped-for introduction of the Arab-Bristol in March 1918 was frustrated. Achieving a satisfactory installation of the Arab proved difficult, and this early attempt, C906, using SE5a (Viper) radiator blocks, was made by the parent Bristol company. (Bristol Aeroplane Co.)

59. Vibration was a major problem in the Sunbeam Arab, and by 10 August 1918 Martlesham had nine Arab-powered F2Bs for testing various engine mountings and installations. One of these is seen here, with short exhaust stubs on the engine but retaining supporting brackets for long horizontal pipes on the fuselage side.

▼ 58

▲60

60. An Arab engine in a Bristol F2B, probably an early installation. Among the various Arab engine mountings tested at Martlesham Heath were one designed at Martlesham itself, a Barnwell, a Standard and two Lanchester designs. A Lanchester mounting was eventually adopted for the production aircraft.

61. Deliveries of production Arab Bristols began in May 1918, these having the form of engine cowling seen here, with long sloping exhaust pipes. By the time of the Armistice, this version of the F2B had, in small numbers, reached several squadrons and the Long-Range Artillery Spotting Flights. The aircraft illustrated is believed to have been assigned to No. 8 Squadron.

62. D7934 was used by L Flight (LRAS Flight) and saw both opera-

tional use and some combat before the war ended. It had been built by the parent British & Colonial Aeroplane Co. (RAF Museum)

63. By 31 December 1918 a total of 1,001 Arab-powered Bristols had been completed. Only 79 had reached France by 31 October 1918, but deliveries continued well into 1919. In the post-Armistice period, No. 59 Squadron replaced its RE8s with Bristols, one of which was E2016, an aircraft built by Armstrong Whitworth. Beside the aircraft is Lt. H. S. R. Burt.

64. A fine study of D7860 (Bristol-built), another of the Arab F2Bs of No. 59 Squadron, seen just airborne at Düren, Germany, in the summer of 1919. (RAF Museum)

▼61

62▲

63▲   64▼

▲65

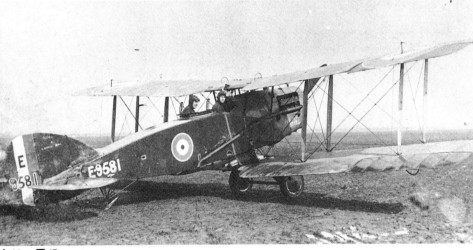

▲66　▼67

65. A near view of the forward fuselage of E2221 (also Bristol-built), aircraft 'C' of No. 36 Training Depot Station, Yatesbury. (RAF Museum)

66. E9581 was one of the 522 Arab Bristols built by the Gloucestershire Aircraft Co. at Sunning-end, Cheltenham, of the 550 ordered from that contractor. The absence of an Aldis sight suggests that the aircraft may have been with a training unit when this photograph was taken. (R. Gerrard)

67. Some Arab-powered Bristol Fighters were supplied to the Training Wing of the Australian Flying Corps at Leighterton. D7955 is known to have been there in December 1918, wearing boomerang markings to proclaim its Australian ownership.

68. The difficulties with the Arab engine made compulsory a search for alternatives. The Siddeley Puma's installation was designed at the Royal Aircraft Establishment, apparently incorporating the suggestions made by Martlesham Heath on 28 February 1918 in Report M.178 on B1206, which had an early and unrelated installation of a Puma (see photograph 56). This photograph of C4655 is dated 24 January 1919; C4654, with Puma, had gone to Martlesham on 14 August 1918. (RAE)

69. Production F2Bs with the Puma did not appear until 1919. This Armstrong Whitworth-built Bristol, E2069, was probably structurally complete in early January but its engine may have been fitted later. The far from complete Ara seen in the background suggests that this photograph dates from early spring 1919. Two later Puma-powered aircraft of this batch, E2089 and E2093, were allocated (but never went) to Poland in March 1920. (Vickers)

▲70

▲71   ▼72

70. Deliveries of Austin-built Bristols started early in July 1919, and 45 had been delivered by 23 August 1919. Numerically, H6058 should have been the 119th aircraft of the batch, but it is uncertain how many were built. It is known that H5952, H5960 and H5963, all Puma-powered, were allocated to Poland in March 1920 but, like E2089 and E2093, did not go there.

71. The upright configuration of the Puma engine necessitated the repositioning of the F2B's Vickers gun. It was mounted to starboard of the engine cylinders, as can just be seen in this photograph of H1690, a Bristol-built aircraft.

72. Another alternative to the Sunbeam Arab was the 200hp Wolseley Viper, and an engine of this type was installed in B1200, which had earlier been fitted with a 200hp Hispano-Suiza. Its Viper installation may have been made at the Southern Aircraft Repair Depot, whence it went to Martlesham Heath for trials on 22

September 1918. It returned to the SARD on 10 October.

73. In pursuance of an early intention to use the air-cooled 200hp RAF (Royal Aircraft Factory) 4d in the Bristol, a specimen engine was sent to the British & Colonial Aeroplane Co. in August 1917. The proposal was abandoned when the Sunbeam Arab was adopted, and only 16 production RAF 4ds were manufactured. Some of these were fitted to F2Bs for experimental purposes at the RAE; a typical installation is seen here.

74. B1201 (seen in photograph 54 with a Hispano-Suiza engine) had its RAF 4d installed by 26 July 1918; it also had the experimental three-bay wings illustrated on F4728 (see photograph 123). This photograph, dated 22 February 1923, shows B1201 with standard mainplanes and its RAF 4d engine. Other Bristols that had the RAF 4d were A7260 and A7860, the latter also having the single-bay wings seen in the illustration of F4360 (photograph 121). (RAE)

▲ 75

▲ 76 ▼ 77

75. With its big air scoop above the engine, the RAF 4d installation lacked elegance and refinement, and A7260's aesthetic appeal was further diminished by the extended heating pipes taken off its exhaust manifolds.

76. Some Bristol Fighters were modified for use as communications aircraft. From these the observer's Scarff ring was removed, and some sketchy provisions were made in the hope of improving the comfort of the occupant of the rear seat. C836, at one time used by No. 9 Squadron RAF, was modified in this way. (D. R. Neate)

77. Some Bristols with wartime training units were given colourful markings. One of the more restrained was the modest checkerboard area painted on C4695, which was aircraft '76' at Marske, the home of No. 2 School of Aerial Fighting and Gunnery and No. 4 Auxiliary School of Aerial Gunnery. On the fuselage side there is a receptacle to catch spent cartridge cases and links from the Vickers gun.

78. More exuberantly checkered was this F2B, reputedly known as 'The Crocodile', doubtless from its fearsome dental décor about the nose. It may have belonged to No. 7 Training Squadron, for it was reported at Netheravon and Witney, successive locations of that unit, and may have been the personal aircraft of a senior instructor or examining officer. So comprehensively was it overpainted that its serial number (possibly C4879) was obliterated.

79, 80. Even more exotic was the elaborate scheme applied to B1288: two photographs are needed to do justice to it. Its squamose splendour was later somewhat dimmed – when it finally crashed the fuselage markings had faded and its fin had apparently been recovered without reinstatement of the fishtail markings. (Chaz Bowyer)

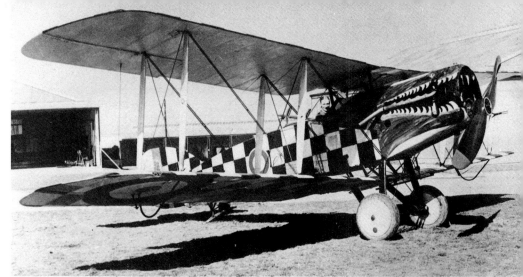

78▲

79▲   80▼

▲81

81. An old warrior that ended its days on training duties was A7237, seen here in 1918 at Amria in Egypt, the home of No. 20 Training Depot Station. The somewhat florid presentation of the serial number was of local creation, and the overall finish may have been experimental or perhaps PC12. A7237 ('Australia No. 9, NSW No. 8') had earlier served operationally with No. 67 Squadron in Palestine.

82. The Bolling Commission recommended that two versions of the Bristol Fighter be produced in the United States for the US Air Service. F2B A7206 was sent to the USA, arriving in New York on 25 August 1917. It was probably the aircraft that was fitted with the first American-made 300hp Hispano-Suiza engine, designated US B-1, and evaluated at McCook Field as P-30 in mid-1918. (National Air & Space Museum)

83. In July 1918 one of the first 290hp Liberty 8 engines was installed in another Bristol-built F2B, which had the McCook Field number P-37. This combination was flying in mid-August, and the aircraft went to Wilbur Wright Field on 6 September. The type had the American designation US B-2.

84. Production of the Bristol Fighter with the 400hp Liberty 12 was ordered from the Curtiss Aeroplane Co. with the American designation USA O-1, but the Liberty installation demanded a structural redesign that led to a runaway increase in weight. The pilot's forward view was severely limited by the bulk and height of the Liberty, and his view for landing must have been partly obstructed by the clumsy flank radiators.

85. A Curtiss-built USA O-1 with the radiator mounted above the leading edge of the centre-section. This arrangement was not adopted, and those O-1s that were built had the flank radiators. Production was suspended when 27 O-1s had been completed, the aircraft having been condemned as unsafe following two fatal crashes.

▼82

▼83

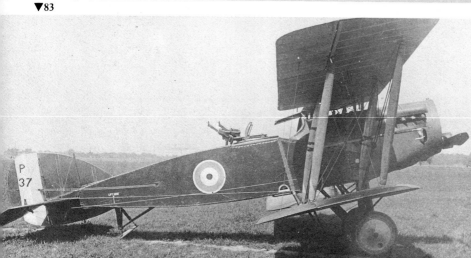

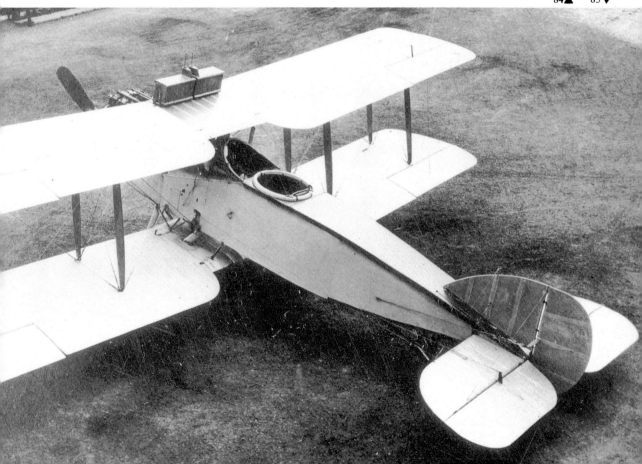

S.C.
40125
X-B-I-A
P
90

▲86 ▼87

F
4425
F·4425
107

86. An American development that was in progress while P-30 and P-37 were being tested was the USXB-1, which had a wooden semi-monocoque fuselage and a 300hp Hispano-Suiza engine. Fuselages were made by the Davies-Putnam Co. and the J. C. Widman Co. This XB-1A, SC40125, was tested at McCook Field as P-90 in 1919–20.

87. In the immediate post-Armistice period, several Bristol Fighter squadrons remained in Germany with the British Army of Occupation. In this photograph, F4425 of No. 48 Squadron is seen in front of the well-known hangars at Bickendorf, near Cologne.

88. Several Bristol Fighter squadrons of the RAF saw service in Ireland during the years following the Armistice. Here are F2Bs of No. 2 Squadron, possibly at Fermoy, Co. Cork, wearing as squadron markings coloured bands around the rear fuselage. (RAF Museum)

88 ▼

89. As early as 24 December 1918, nine Bristol Fighters had been assigned to No. 11 Group for No. 105 Squadron. F4801 was not one of the original nine, but it was with No. 105 Squadron at Gormanston, Co. Meath, in February 1919. (RAF Museum)

90. F4796 was the first Bristol Fighter to be delivered to No. 106 Squadron at Collinstown, Westmeath.

91, 92. Some of No. 106 Squadron's Bristols had spectacular paint schemes while at Fermoy. In July 1919, F4380 had been on the strength of No. 11 Group in Ireland, and was flown by Lt. Col. (later Gp. Capt.) G. I. Carmichael DSO. With No. 106 Squadron, however, F4380 bore markings that may have been an attempt at a form of dazzle painting. The 'sunburst' on the upper wing and fuselage sides, and the liberal striping elsewhere on H1441 (also of No. 106 Squadron), suggest a more personal flamboyance – perhaps that of Flt. Lt. Waller, believed to have been F4380's pilot at the time.

93. In January 1919, an official request was made for three Bristol Fighters, H1687–1689, to be delivered from current production as two-seat communications aircraft with dual controls and increased tankage to provide five hours endurance. The second of these was H1688, which had an open cockpit for the passenger. Although lacking H1460's enclosed coupé top, it had deckings ahead of and behind the rear cockpit.

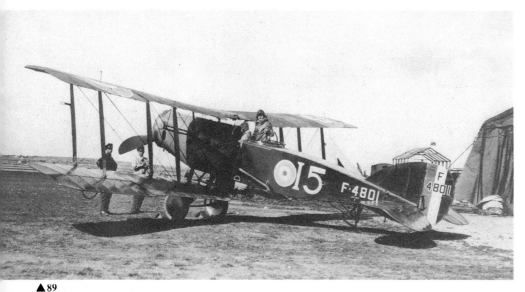

▲89

▲90 ▼91

▲94

▲95   ▼96

94. The three officially requested communications Bristols were preceded by the rather more refined H1460, which gave its passenger greater comfort in a better-appointed cockpit under a hinged coupé top. It was purchased by the Air Board on 19 May 1919, and on at least one occasion was flown in the company of a formation of standard F2Bs of No. 24 Squadron.
95. During the 1920s, the basic design was progressively developed. J6586, designated Bristol Fighter Mk. II and seen here at Martlesham, was built new late in 1919 with desert equipment and a so-called tropical cooling system, with service in the Middle East and India in view. It was effectively a prototype for over 400 similar Bristols that gave sterling service as general-purpose and army-co-operation aircraft for many years.

96. The standard Bristol Fighter Mk. IV had the strengthened fuse-lage and revised vertical tail surfaces, but the upper mainplane reverted to being of standard F2B planform, with the addition of Handley Page slots. F4587, seen here at Martlesham Heath, came on to the British civil register in 1938 as G-AFHJ. It was destroyed during the 1939–45 war.
97. No. 4 Squadron's Bristols were transported to the Middle East aboard the aircraft carrier *Argus* in October 1922 for operations necessitated by the Chanak crisis. Here J6761 is given attention on *Argus'* flight deck.
98. In this photograph, which bears the date 11 October 1922, one of No. 4 Squadron's Bristols is seen taking off from *Argus*. (K. M. Molson)

THIS MACHINE MUST NOT BE
FLOWN WITHOUT PASSENGER
OR EQUIVALENT IN WEIGHT
IN GUNNERS COCKPIT

99. H1420 had a redesigned structure capable of taking heavier loads and was a conversion of a more basic F2B. It was photographed at Filton in March 1926, with the ultimate in extended exhaust pipes, an oleo tailskid, a message pick-up hook, and sundry other impedimenta. Officially regarded as the prototype Bristol Fighter Mk. III, it was sufficiently different from the basic design to merit the new Bristol type number 96. (Bristol Aeroplane Co.)

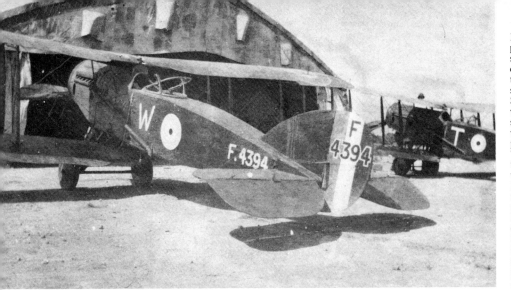

▲100

▲101 ▼102

100. Many F2Bs of wartime production remained in service, or were brought out of store to serve, long after the war ended. F4394 is seen here with No. 5 Squadron in India, still in wartime PC10 finish and still fitted with the final wartime form of exhaust pipes. Although marked 'W', this Bristol also bore the identifying letter 'N' while with No. 5 Squadron.
101. By 1924, when this air-to-air photograph was taken, the RAF's Bristol Fighters had the standard overall aluminium finish. D8036, another F2B of wartime origin, was at that time aircraft 'H' of No. 5 Squadron. (P. H. T. Green)
102. When photographed at Mosul, Iraq, in June 1929, F4686 of No. 6 Squadron had underwing panniers into which luggage or other freight could be placed. The resultant drag must have taxed the long-suffering Bristol close to the limits of aerodynamic acceptability, and this aircraft's adjustable-pitch propeller cannot have been any compensation. (P. H. T. Green)
103. The fin marking on D7812 suggests that it may have been with No. 13 Squadron when this photograph was taken. This well-groomed and obviously cherished Bristol had highly polished engine-cowling panels.
104. Among the aircraft present when the airfield at Jerusalem was opened in May 1924 were these Bristol Fighters of No. 14 Squadron: J6593 (left) and J6648 (right). (P. Liddle)
105. This study of F4839 (No. 20 Squadron) eloquently testifies to the overburdening of the RAF's Bristol Fighters in the late 1920s. The aircraft exhibits most of the drag-creating accretions in the inventory: full-length exhaust pipes, supplementary radiator, tropical header tank, external bomb sight, message hook, Holt flare brackets, navigation lights, Handley Page slots, trailing-aerial sinker weight, and doubtless others not visible in this photograph.

103▲

104▲ 105▼

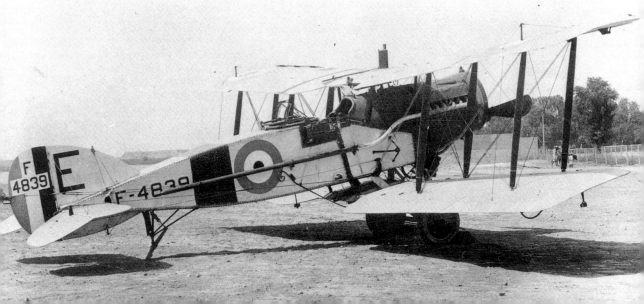

▲106   ▼107

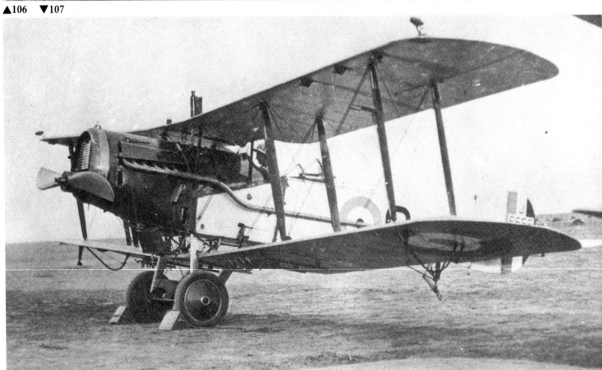

50

106. Maintenance of the ageing Bristols in the postwar RAF under scandalous financial restrictions taxed the ingenuity and dedication of the ground staff. Here, an aircraft of No. 20 Squadron is being worked on. The supplementary radiator and its plumbing can be seen, as can the underwing bomb racks, whilst the box-like oil tank, removed from the starboard side of the engine, is lying on the ground in front of the starboard wheel.

107. Photographed at Risalpur in 1930, J6656 was aircraft 'G' of No. 28 Squadron. In general appearance and equipment, it resembles F4839 of No. 20 Squadron (see photograph 105).

108. Several years earlier, still in PC10 finish and unencumbered with the excrescences that came with the passage of time and developments in operational demands, E2450 of No. 31 Squadron was photographed at Lahore.

109. Another Bristol Fighter squadron that went to Turkey at the time of the Chanak crisis was No. 208. In this photograph, some of its aircraft are seen at San Stefano, the nearest being H1623, H1501 and H1678. Of these, H1501 was also reported at No. 4 Flying Training School, Abu Sueir, Egypt, in September 1922.

110. At a different time and place, D7819 of No. 208 Squadron displays an individual marking on its fin. (A. Thomas)

108 ▲

109 ▲   110 ▼

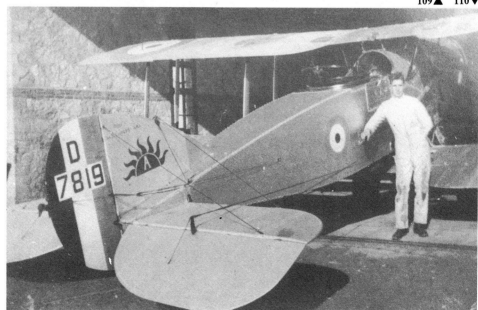

▲111

▲112 ▼113

52

111. This Bristol had the adjustable pitch propeller that was fitted to many of its kind in the hope of improving the aircraft's performance.

112. In the twilight of its RAF career, this Bristol found prosaic ground-borne employment as an instructional airframe at RAF Halton, its original identity replaced by the marking 'Instr. 213M'. The airframe appears to be essentially that of the wartime Bristol Fighter, and it has the final war-time exhaust pipes.

113. A few Bristol Fighters were hurled sacrificially to watery ends as catapult dummies, as were several time-expired DH9As. This photograph depicts the launching of a Bristol from the catapult ship *Ark Royal* on 27 March 1930.

114. Several Bristol Fighters were employed to test experimental and exploratory installations of parachutes from 1918 onwards. In tests of the Calthrop A1 parachute at the Royal Aircraft Establishment at Farnborough, A7260 and H1561 were used. This photograph, dated 21 September 1918, shows a Calthrop installation on a Bristol Fighter at the Isle of Grain, with a dummy bomb serving as weight. The external stowage was necessitated by the parachute's static-line method of opening.

115. With employment in the heat of India and the Middle East imminent in the postwar period, attention was given to improving the cooling of the Bristol's Falcon. Several aircraft had this large-area, flat-topped radiator, which so reduced forward view that it would have been unacceptable in France. This aircraft appears to be D8074 and bears the individual marking '20'. Another seen in the Middle East was D8037.

116. Another F2B with the large-area radiator, photographed at the Isle of Grain.

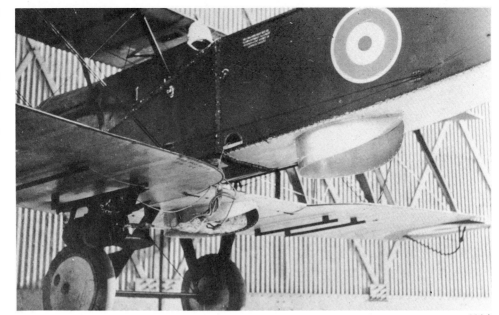
114▲

115▲ 116▼

▲117

117. The RAE's experiments in cooling installations included this liberally-vented cowling behind a seemingly standard radiator. The aircraft may have been C4654, and the photograph bears the date 29 April 1923. (RAE)

118. J6800, a Mk. II, was tested at Martlesham Heath with a long-range fuel tank mounted under the lower centre-section.

119. J6790, another Mk. II of the same post-Armistice production batch, photographed at Filton in 1920, with an oleo undercarriage

▼118

and large-section ('desert') tyres. Although not adopted for RAF Bristol Fighters, oleo undercarriages of similar form were fitted to some of the aircraft supplied to Belgium and Spain. (Bristol Aeroplane Co.)

120. The Royal Aircraft Establishment also used the Bristol Fighter in tests of experimental exhaust pipes. Here, C4654 sports what seems to be an experimental silencer with a slipstream-assisted exhaust pipe. (RAE)

▲121

121. From July 1918, Farnborough conducted investigations into the lift and drag of the Bristol Fighter with wings of three different aspect ratios. These were the standard 39ft 3in wings, single-bay wings 30ft 11½in in span and 7ft in chord, and three-bay wings spanning 44ft 1½in and of 4ft 9in chord. Here, in January 1923, F4360 wears the single-bay wings. (RAE)

122. An exactly contemporary photograph of F4728 illustrates the long-span, three-bay mainplanes; on both these aircraft there were strut-like links between upper and lower ailerons. The results of the RAE investigations were published in 1923 in Reports & Memoranda No. 859: *Lift and drag of the Bristol Fighter with wings of three aspect ratios.* (RAE)

122▼

123. A Bristol Fighter fitted with a four-blade all-metal propeller of Air Ministry design and possibly of adjustable pitch, and with bomb racks under the lower wings and centre-section. This photograph may have been taken at Martlesham Heath.

124. That directional control of the much-cluttered Bristol Fighters of the 1920s became impaired is indicated in the revised vertical tail assembly of the Mk. IV version (see photos 1 and 96). The RAE evidently took a hand in related investigations and tried out this rather elegant upper fin and horn-balanced rudder on C4776. This photograph is dated 23 March 1925. (RAE)

125. Possibly Farnborough's most elaborate Bristol-based creation was the barely recognizable J6721, which had mainplanes of steel construction and RAF 34 section, enclosing leading-edge condensers for the experimental evaporative cooling system of the modified Falcon. The engine drove a Leitner-Watts adjustable-pitch propeller. The photograph is dated 6 October 1930. (RAE)

126, 127. His and hers: two Falcon-powered Bristol Fighters for the King and Queen of the Belgians. King Albert's aircraft (photo 126), which bears a suitably regal monogram on the fuselage, was presented to him by Handley Page on 14 May 1920; after modifications requested by the King it was flown back to Brussels on 23 July 1920. The aircraft presented to the Queen (127) was a gift from the Aircraft Disposals Co. (owned by Handley Page), and was flown from Croydon to Brussels by Capt. Muir. It appears to have been G-EBCU, ex-E2058, delivered to Brussels on 6 May 1922.

▲123　▼124

125▲

126▲   127▼

▲128

128. Perhaps inspired by the two F2Bs presented to the King and Queen of the Belgians, Belgium purchased fifteen Bristols with the 300hp Hispano-Suiza from the Aircraft Disposals Co. and sixteen new-built aircraft, similarly powered, from the Bristol company. One of the latter is seen here at Filton before delivery in 1921. (Bristol Aeroplane Co.)

129. Additionally, forty Bristol Fighters with the 300hp Hispano-Suiza were built under licence in Belgium in 1925 by the Société Anonyme Belge de Constructions Aéronautiques. This Bristol had the Belgian number '45' and may have been SABCA-built. When

photographed it had an oleo undercarriage and the horn-balanced rudder and fin of the British Mk. IVs.

130. Perhaps the greatest fighting exponent of the Bristol F2B was Maj. A. E. McKeever, a Canadian officer who served with No. 11 Squadron RFC and amassed a victory score of 30 by the end of 1917. When he was appointed to the command of No. 1 Squadron of the Canadian Air Force in November 1918, he was given F4336 as his personal aircraft, and this machine subsequently went to Canada to become G-CYBC on 6 August 1920.

▼129

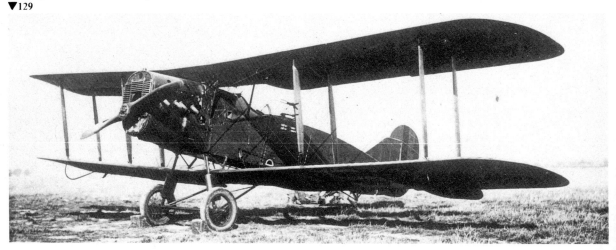

130▼

▲131
131. After the ex-RAF Bristols H1557 and H1558 had been given to New Zealand under the Imperial Gift scheme, five more were ordered as new aircraft. In service with the NZ Permanent Air Force, they wore their Bristol works sequence numbers as service numbers, as seen here on 6856, the first of the five, photographed at Wigram in about 1927. (D. P. Woodhall)

132. The RAF did not use any Bristol Fighter with the 300hp Hispano-Suiza engine, but this version was offered by the Aircraft Disposals Co. The photograph is believed to show one of the company's demonstration Bristols. (RAF Museum)

133. The Bristol company built new F2Bs with the 300hp Hispano-Suiza: this aircraft, one of five supplied to Spain in 1921, was photographed at Filton after completion. The engine installation, cowling and radiator were essentially similar to those fitted to wartime Arab-powered Bristols. (Bristol Aeroplane Co.)

134

134. The aircraft of a later batch of twelve supplied to Spain had the 300hp Hispano-Suiza (with stub exhausts on this example at least), an oleo undercarriage and Frise balanced ailerons. (Bristol Aeroplane Co.)

▼135

135. One of six standard Falcon-powered Bristol F2B Mk IIs supplied to the Irish Free State in 1925. In Irish Army service these aircraft bore the identifying numbers 17–22. (Bristol Aeroplane Co.)